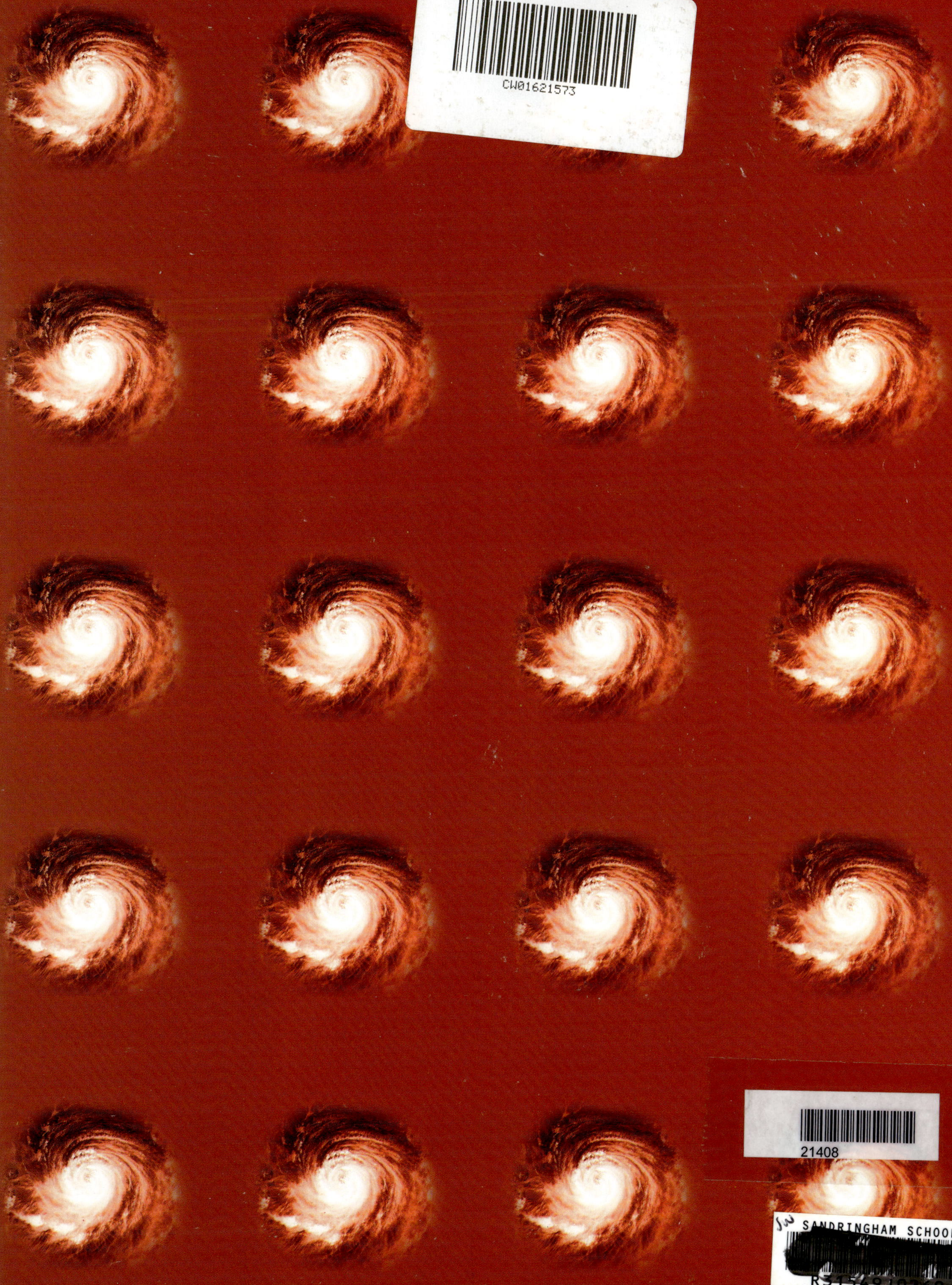

Picture credits:
t=top b=bottom m=middle l=left r=right c=centre
National Aeronautics and Space Administration (NASA): 7b, 14t, 17b, 38l
National Oceanic and Atmospheric Administration (NOAA): 11r, 12l, 14m, 14bl, 22l, 24b, 17m, 31b, 32t, 32l, 33br, 37m, 37b, 38br
Digital Globe: 12r
Dave Gatley/FEMA News: 17m, 21m, 33bl, 34b, 41b
FEMA News: 18t, 20b
Dave Saville/FEMA News: 19b, 19m
Bob Epstein/FEMA News: 18c
Mark Wolfe/FEMA News: 22t
Bob McMillan/FEMA News: 28t
Andrea Booher/FEMA News: 29b, 29t
Liz Roll/FEMA News: 30t
Adam Dubrowa/FEMA News: 30b, 31m
Patricia Brach/FEMA News: 41m
Jason Pack/FEMA News: 40b
Leif Skoogfors/FEMA News: 40t

Published By: Robert Frederick Ltd.
4 North Parade Bath, England.
First Published: 2005

Designed and packaged by
Q2A Creative
Printed in India

HURRICANES & TORNADOES

CONTENTS

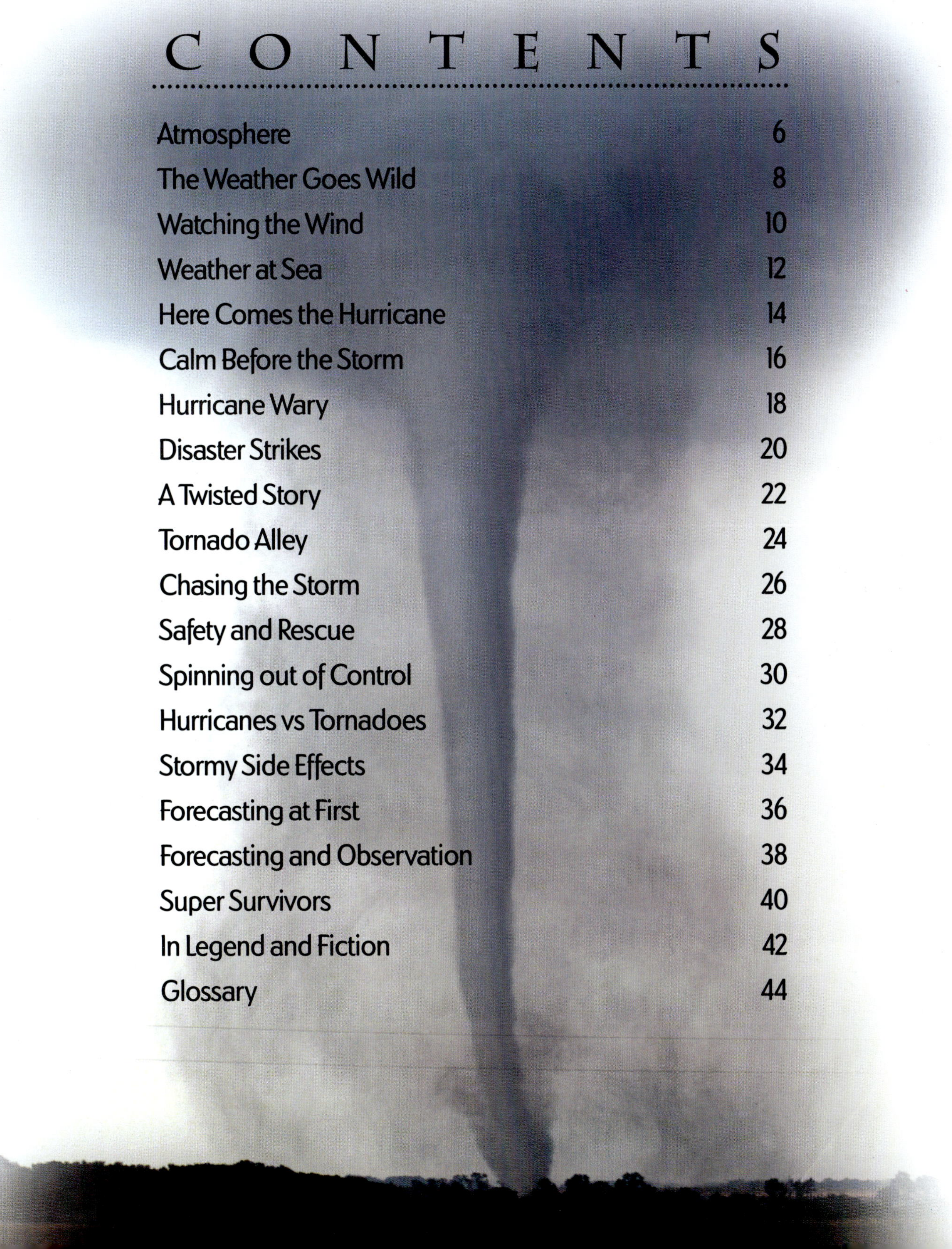

Atmosphere

The Earth is surrounded by a thin blanket of air called the atmosphere, which is held in place by the Earth's gravity. The atmosphere absorbs the Sun's energy, preventing too much heat from entering the Earth. It also recycles water.

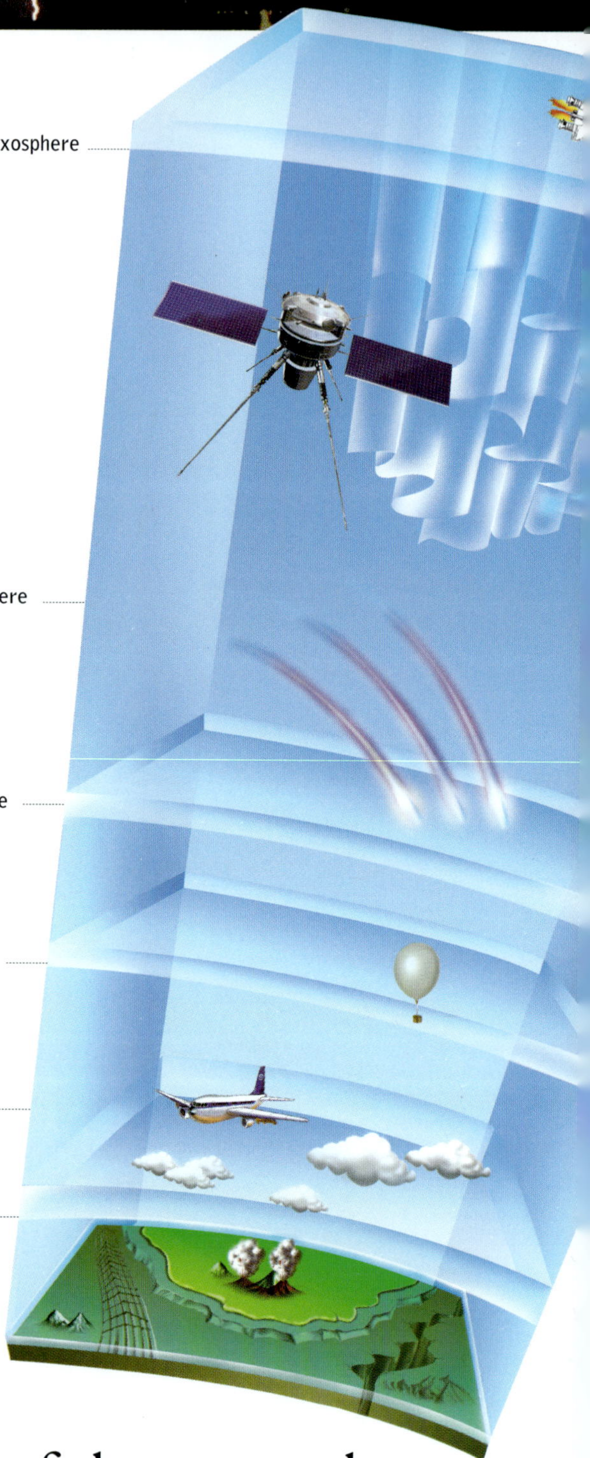

Weather

Weather is the state of the Earth's atmosphere at a particular time over a particular place. It occurs because the atmosphere is forever changing. Factors that influence weather include temperature, air pressure, wind, clouds and precipitation.

▲ *Pollution from industries and vehicles is causing a rise in the Earth's temperature. This phenomena of global warming is affecting weather patterns drastically, causing excessive floods, drought and heat waves*

Layers of the atmosphere

Based on temperature and density, the Earth's atmosphere is divided into five layers: troposphere, stratosphere, mesosphere, thermosphere and exosphere. The troposphere is where all weather changes take place. Clouds and storms are formed here.

▲ *An aneroid barograph records changes in the atmospheric pressure*

INTERESTING FACT

All living things need oxygen to breathe. However, oxygen makes up only 21 per cent of the Earth's atmosphere. The atmosphere mainly consists of nitrogen, which accounts for about 78 per cent of the total gas present in the atmosphere!

FACT FILE

REGIONS OF THE ATMOSPHERE

- **Troposphere:** About 10-13 km (6-8 miles) above the Earth's surface
- **Stratosphere:** From a lower boundary of about 6-17 km (4-11 miles) to a higher border at about 50 km (30 miles)
- **Mesosphere:** Between about 50 km (30 miles) and 80 km (50 miles)
- **Thermosphere:** Between about 80 km (50 miles) and 450 km (280 miles)
- **Exosphere:** Begins at an altitude of about 500 km (300 miles)

Air pressure

The air molecules in the atmosphere exert weight on the surroundings. This weight is known as pressure and it depends on the amount of molecules present and their speed. As we go up, the number of molecules decreases, thus reducing the pressure. Air pressure also changes with the temperature. A rise in temperature will usually lower the air pressure.

Air mass

A large body of air that exhibits uniform temperature and humidity is called an air mass. The property of an air mass depends on the source region. Air mass over polar regions is normally cold and dry. When an air mass moves from the source region, it will meet another mass with different properties.

► *The boundary between two air masses is called a front. Cold fronts are responsible for stormy weather*

The Weather Goes Wild

Blizzards, thunderstorms, hurricanes, heat waves, droughts and hailstorms are some examples of extreme or severe weather conditions. We are all fascinated – and also a little scared – when the weather goes wild. Extreme weather events can damage property and crops, and even endanger our lives.

When the negatively charged particles in a thunderstorm meet the positively charged particles on the ground, a channel is formed. Electric current passing through this channel forces air molecules to release light. This is how lightning occurs

Unpredictable weather

The atmosphere is in constant motion, making the weather largely unpredictable. Apart from temperature, precipitation (rain, snow, or hail), wind speed and atmospheric pressure, the Earth's tilt as it revolves around the Sun also causes changes in weather. The study of weather is known as meteorology and scientists who study and predict weather are called meteorologists.

The water droplets on the top of thunderstorm clouds freeze to form ice crystals. Sometimes, these ice crystals melt to fall down as rain. At other times, they grow in size and come down as hailstones

Thunderstorm

A thunderstorm includes thunder and lightning, and usually rain or hail. Most thunderstorms are not destructive. However, severe ones can lead to floods and cause fires. Sometimes, thunderstorms can even produce tornadoes. Thunderstorms usually occur during spring and summer. Most of these violent storms strike in the afternoon or evening.

Severe thunderstorm

The humidity in rising warm air condenses to form clouds, ice crystals and rain, resulting in a thunderstorm. However, upper-air disturbances, which are pools of cold air moving along with the winds, may provide a lifting motion to produce an unusually strong thunderstorm

INTERESTING FACT

In 1993, from March 12 to 15, an unusually powerful nor'easter produced a trail of snow, flooding and hurricane-force winds in the eastern United States. From Alabama to Maine, it was a time of record-smashing cold temperatures. Florida was hit by tornadoes. In all, over 235 people died and damages worth more than $1 billion were incurred. No wonder, the storm earned the epithet "Storm of the Century"!

FACT FILE

Meteorologists define weather as 'severe' when one of the following things happens:

- **Hail** 2 cm (¾ inch) in diameter, or larger;
- **Wind gusts** 25 metres per second (58 miles per hour), or more;
- **Wind** causes damage such as the uprooting of trees and the destruction of homes and buildings;
- A **storm** occurs

Winter storms

Winter storms may bring snow, freezing rain or sleet, and ice. They include blizzards, ice storms and 'nor'easters' (strong northeasterly winds). Winter storms often create havoc, disrupting normal life and activities. Heavy snowfall can reduce visibility, making driving during snowstorms dangerous.

Blizzards are severe snowstorms accompanied by strong winds. People and animals can get buried in piles of snow during blizzards

Heat wave

'Heat wave' is a term used to describe extraordinarily hot weather over a long period. One of the main reasons for heat waves is global warming, or excessive heating of the Earth's surface. Heat waves can cause heat strokes, at times even leading to death. Sometimes heat waves are accompanied by drought.

Watching the Wind

Wind refers to the movement of air over the Earth's surface. It is usually caused by differences in temperature and unequal heating of the Earth's surface. When the Sun heats up a certain area, the air above that place is also heated. The warm air rises, and cool air comes in to take its place. This movement creates winds.

▲ *Winds are also caused by the Earth's rotation and differences in atmospheric pressure. Wind always flows from a point of high pressure to a point of low pressure*

▲ *The anemometer is the most widely used instrument for measuring wind speeds*

Measuring the wind

Meteorologists use various instruments to study winds and to measure their speed, direction, temperature and pressure. Surface winds are measured by wind vanes and anemometers. Winds higher up in the atmosphere are studied using pilot balloons or aircraft reports.

Beaufort wind scale

Sir Francis Beaufort (1777-1857) of the British Royal Navy devised a system of estimating wind speeds. The Beaufort force or number combines the wind speed with the visible effects of the wind on land objects and/or sea surfaces. The numbers range from 0 to 12, going from calm air and breeze to strong winds or gales.

Coriolis effect

As the Earth spins, winds tend to move to the right in the Northern Hemisphere, and to the left in the Southern Hemisphere. This movement of winds is called the Coriolis effect. It has a great influence on weather patterns.

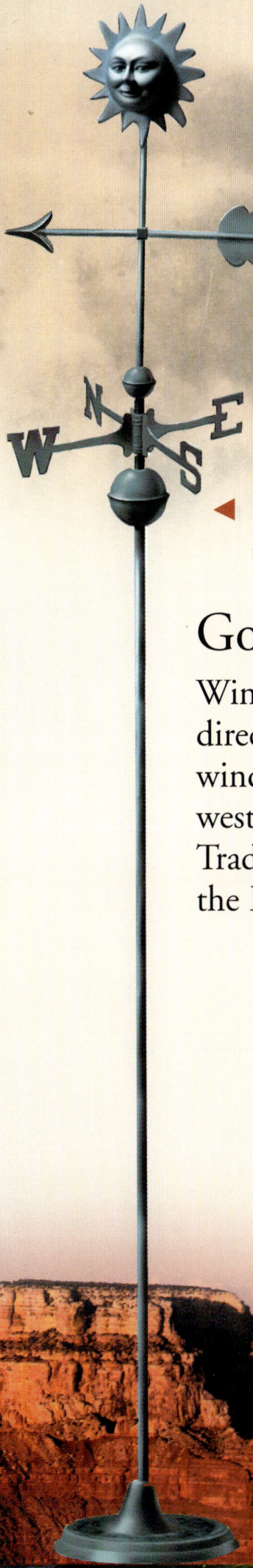

◄ *Wind vanes on top of barns and houses tell us in which direction the wind is blowing*

Going in different directions

Winds are also classified according to the direction from which they blow. Easterly winds blow from east to west, while the westerly ones blow from west to east. Trade winds are steady and flow towards the Equator.

INTERESTING FACT

Air from high-pressure areas flow towards low-pressure areas. Since the pressure changes so quickly, the air travels at high speeds between areas of different pressures, forming strong winds. These winds, which can reach speeds of over 320 kilometres per hour (199 mph), are called jet streams.

FACT FILE

BEAUFORT SCALE NUMBER	DESCRIPTIVE TERM
0	Calm
1-3	Light winds
4	Moderate winds
5	Fresh winds
6	Strong winds
7	Near gale
8	Gale
9	Strong gale
10	Storm
11	Violent storm
12+	Hurricane

► *Strong winds blowing over dry land can cause dust storms*

▼ *Severe wind and sand erosion have curved the splendid sandstone rocks at Utah, U.S.*

Weather at Sea

Sailors often face dangerous and life-threatening weather at sea. They must cope with tidal waves, tsunamis, tornadoes and tropical storms. The effects of such severe weather are also felt on land, where immense loss of life and property can occur.

▲ *Tidal waves are not destructive like 'free waves', but one must keep away from beaches, coves and sea caves during high tides since the chances of drowning are very high*

Tidal wave

A tidal wave is a sea wave caused by tidal forces. It is usually used to refer to the huge swelling of the ocean surface on either side of the Earth. It is caused by the gravitational forces of the Sun and the Moon, and not by earthquakes – as many people wrongly believe. The wave produced by an earthquake is called a 'free wave'.

Tsunami

A tsunami (from the Japanese *tsu* for 'harbour' and *nami* for 'wave') is a large, destructive wave. It is very different from a tidal wave. A tsunami may be caused by earthquakes, submarine landslides, volcanic eruptions and even meteorite strikes. As the wave heads toward the shore, it gains height and speed. By the time it hits the shore, the tsunami may become a 30-metre (100-feet) tall crest.

► *A tsunami travels outward from its starting point – much like the ripples in a pond, until it hits the shore*

Tropical storms

A tropical cyclone is a violent, tropical weather system in which the air in the centre is warmer than the surrounding winds. These storms go through many stages as they develop, and each has a life span of several days. They are accompanied by very heavy rain, thunder and lightning.

INTERESTING FACT

The tsunami that hit the Southeast and South Asian countries around the Indian Ocean on December 26, 2004, was generated by an earthquake measuring 9.2 on the Richter scale. It literally shook the world. A NASA geophysicist reported that the planet tilted about 2.5 cm (0.9 inches) on its axis and spun three microseconds faster.

FACT FILE

A TSUNAMI CAN

- Travel as quickly as a jet plane (more than 640 km/h or 400 mph)
- Travel unobserved on the surface of deep seas, at speeds up to 800 km/h or 500 mph
- Have a wavelength of up to 1000 km, or 600 miles
- Comprise a set of waves that may last for several hours
- Be as high as 30 metres (100 feet)

MOST ACTIVE TSUNAMI ZONE

- The Pacific

Lighthouses warn ships of dangers like rocks and low water levels. They also help to show the way during storms and heavy rains

Anchored buoys are used for weather observation in the sea. Each buoy is equipped with instruments that record and monitor weather developments

Here comes the Hurricane

Hurricanes are large, rotating storms that form over warm oceans near the Equator. These tropical storms may have wind speeds of 119 km/h (74 mph). They are called 'hurricanes' in the Atlantic and eastern Pacific oceans, 'typhoons' in the North Pacific and the Philippines, and 'cyclones' in the Indian and South Pacific oceans.

Seasonal occurrences

Hurricanes mostly occur between June and November. Although meteorologists have the basic knowledge of where and when hurricanes can occur, they are unable to predict the exact location of a hurricane before it develops. Hence, a hurricane's path can be forecast only after it is formed.

Christening a hurricane

All hurricanes are given names that help us identify and track them as they move across the ocean. Short, easy names are chosen to avoid confusion when two or more hurricanes occur at the same time.

◀ *A specialist group of pilots, called Hurricane Hunters, fly into the hurricane to gather valuable information that help scientists predict its size, strength and future path*

▲ *Satellite photograph of a hurricane*

Hurricane names

The current system of naming hurricanes was adopted in 1979. The World Meteorological Organization chooses hurricane names from lists that are used in rotation. The Atlantic is assigned six lists of names, with one list used each year. Names of huge, destructive hurricanes are 'retired', never to be used again.

◀ *A 1949 hurricane was named Bess after the wife of the then U.S. president, Harry Truman*

INTERESTING FACT

The word 'hurricane' is believed to have its origin in the Caribbean islands. The tropical cyclone is believed to have been named after the Carib god of evil and violent storms, Hurican.

FACT FILE

- Clement Wragge, an Australian meteorologist, began giving women's names to tropical storms before the end of the 19th century
- In 1953, the U.S. National Weather Service began using female names for storms
- In 1979, both women's and men's names were used
- One name for each letter of the alphabet is selected, except for Q, U, X, Y and Z

Hurricane alert

When the weather bureau is certain that a hurricane is about to strike, it puts out a warning in the coastal areas where very strong winds and high waves are expected. The public is informed through television and radio broadcasts, and also by means of flying flags and lights.

▶ *A pair of square red banners, each with black squares in the middle, are used to warn of hurricanes. These flags are replaced at night by two red lights with a white light placed in-between*

Hurricane Wary

Hurricanes can cause immense destruction to life and property. Thanks to satellites, though, scientists can now track hurricanes and issue watches and warnings. A 'watch' cautions that a hurricane is possible within 36 hours, while a 'warning' means that severe weather is already present and there is imminent danger.

▲ *Sometimes coastal and low-lying inland areas need to be evacuated due to heavy rains, flash floods and storm surges. In such cases, shelter camps are set up to accommodate those who have lost their homes*

Getting ready for the storm

You may not be able to leave home for a few days. Hence, a disaster kit containing bottled water, canned food, a radio for news, batteries for flashlights, and medical supplies is a must. Shut off utilities like electricity and gas. Make sure the car has petrol so that you can leave at any time. If there are no evacuation orders, stay indoors. If the wind stops, do not think the storm is over. It could be the eye of the storm, and the winds will come again.

Protecting your house

Houses in hurricane-prone areas have special features to protect against high winds and flooding. They are elevated on stilts, so that they are above the high water that hurricanes bring.

▲ *Hurricane straps keep roofs attached to walls, while storm shutters protect windows and glass from flying debris like tree trunks and other objects carried by strong winds*

An emergency plan for pets

Disasters like hurricanes and floods affect animals as well. Pets get scared and upset during storms, and they may get injured or stranded. Not all emergency shelters allow animals, so special arrangements need to be made to take care of them.

Listening to the weather radio

Weather radios broadcast warnings and watches 24 hours a day. Most weather radios run on batteries. They send out a special alarm tone even when switched off, to alert people about dangerous weather – giving them enough time to take shelter.

INTERESTING FACT

In the United States, the Federal Emergency Management Agency (FEMA) runs an Urban Search and Rescue system to help people during emergencies like hurricanes. Specially trained dogs are a part of this team. They help locate and rescue people trapped under collapsed buildings, trees or other debris.

FACT FILE

- A typical hurricane brings at least 6-12 inches (0.5-1 foot) of rainfall, often resulting in severe flooding
- Inland flooding has been the primary cause of tropical cyclone-related fatalities over the past 30 years
- In the 20th century, 23 hurricanes have each caused damage in excess of $1 billion

▲ *Trained teams search for, and rescue, animals that get stranded during natural disasters*

Disaster Strikes

Tropical cyclones are the largest and most destructive storms on Earth. At sea, hurricanes spawn powerful winds and tremendous waves. They lead to storm surges – the piling up of water at a storm's centre – that can raise the sea level more than 6 metres (20 feet), and even drown a coastline. Heavy rains can cause inland floods and landslides.

▲ *Storm surges generated by hurricanes cause immense damage on land*

Hurricane Andrew, 1992

The costliest U.S. natural disaster was Hurricane Andrew. This deadly storm hit South Florida, causing $26.5 billion in damages.

Killer storm surges

The deadliest natural disaster in U.S. history was the 1900 Galveston, Texas, hurricane, which killed an estimated 8,000 people. Most of the deaths were caused by the storm surge. The 1970 cyclone that hit East Pakistan (present-day Bangladesh) caused a storm surge that left about 500,000 people dead.

▲ *Manatees usually locate sheltered areas near the shore during hurricanes*

INTERESTING FACT

In Florida, U.S., manatee deaths caused by boat collisions during 2004 were the lowest in five years. Biologists believe this could be due to the four hurricanes that hit the Florida coast within six weeks – keeping people out of the sea. Only 69 manatees were killed by boats in 2004, as compared to 95 in 2002.

FACT FILE

- **Hurricane David, 1979:** Dominican Republic; winds 277 km/hr (172 mph); 1,300 dead
- **Hurricane Andrew, 1992:** Florida, Louisiana and the Bahamas; winds 270 km/hr (168 mph); over 50 dead
- **Hurricane Mitch, 1998:** Central America; winds 290 km/hr (180 mph); about 11,000 dead
- **Hurricane Floyd, 1999:** United States; winds 250 km/hr (155 mph); some 3 million people evacuated in the largest peacetime exercise of its type in American history

Hurricane Mitch, 1998

Hurricane Mitch was the deadliest Atlantic hurricane since 1780. It raged for 13 days over the Caribbean Sea and the Bahamas. The floods and landslides killed about 11,000 people in Central America, while another 3 million were left homeless.

◀ *Hurricanes cause torrential rains, leading to landslides and floods*

Hurricane Floyd, 1999

Hurricane Floyd devastated hundreds of miles of the east coast of the United States, from Florida to Maine, causing about $6 billion in flood damage. Most of the 56 deaths were caused by flooding.

◀ *Hurricanes with their storm surges, winds and flooding can cause untold damage*

A Twisted Story

Tornadoes are violent storms that look like black, funnel-shaped clouds. The wind in these storms can reach a speed of 500km/hr (310 mph). Tornadoes are capable of destroying everything in their path.

▲ *The most violent tornadoes (F5) can uproot houses and trees*

A super tornado

Most severe tornadoes originate in rotating thunderstorms, which form in regions where cold, dry polar winds mix with warm, moist tropical air. These thunderstorms are called supercells, and are characterised by rotating winds, called 'mesocyclone', rising into the storm. The mesocyclone is a spine of wind that spins through the supercells. The wind starts to swirl fast to form a funnel. As the air in the funnel spins faster, it creates a low-pressure area that sucks in air and objects.

◀ *Supercells can come together in a huge cluster and develop a mesocyclone. As the mesocyclone gathers force, it starts to spin faster and extends further towards the ground to form a giant tornado. However, not all mesocyclones produce tornadoes*

Tornado season

Tornadoes can occur at any time of the year. In the southern states of the United States, the peak tornado season is March through May – with May having the most. In the northern states, the peak months are during the summer.

INTERESTING FACT

Tornadoes can be very strong. There are instances where tornadoes have lifted trees from one place and deposited them hundreds of miles away. A tornado in Minnesota lifted a train almost 25 metres (80 feet) into the air!

FACT FILE

- On an annual average, the United States experiences 100,000 thunderstorms, resulting in over 1,000 tornadoes and about 50 deaths. Most of these are F0 and F1 tornadoes
- F5 tornadoes account for less than 2 per cent of all tornadoes in the United States
- On average, 33 tornadoes are reported each year in the United Kingdom

Striking in the dark

The thunderstorms that produce tornadoes usually take place in the afternoon. Tornadoes are most likely to occur between 3.00 p.m. and 9.00 p.m., but can take place at all hours of the day or night.

Tornado classification

In 1971, Tetsuya Theodore Fujita created the Fujita Tornado Intensity Scale, which ranks tornadoes by the damage they cause to manmade structures. The tornadoes are ranked on an increasing scale from F0 to F5. The numbers are ratings of tornado wind speed.

T. Fujita introduced the concept of tornado families, each family including specific tornadoes produced by the same thunderstorm – but with separate paths

Tornado Alley

Compared with other kinds of storms, tornadoes are rare. That is probably the reason why scientists still do not fully understand how tornadoes form, grow and die. Tornadoes can last from a few seconds to more than an hour. They might remain on the ground for just a few yards, or stretch across more than 160 kilometres (100 miles).

Waterspout

A waterspout is a tornado that passes over water. It is a funnel-shaped storm consisting of wind, water and ocean spray. It is generally weaker than a land tornado. Waterspouts occur most frequently in warm tropical waters.

▼ *Sometimes, waterspouts can move over land and cause considerable damage. In fact, many of the tornadoes along the Gulf Coast originate in the Gulf of Mexico as waterspouts*

Tornado Alley

Some regions of the world have a higher frequency of tornadoes than others. One such place is the Tornado Alley in the United States, and refers to the region on the Great Plains extending from central Texas to the Canadian border. The conditions there favour the formation of the most severe tornadoes in spring and early summer, earning it the name Tornado Alley.

▲ *Tornadoes are most frequent in Tornado Alley during April-June, with the highest occurrence in Oklahoma, Texas and Florida*

INTERESTING FACT

The word 'tornado' has been derived from the Spanish 'tornear', meaning to turn, or twist. Tornadoes are formed by rotating winds, and hence the name. Tornadoes are also called 'twisters' for the same reason.

FACT FILE

- Tornadoes have hit all 50 states in the United States, though this does not happen every year
- Tornadoes are most common in the spring and early summer
- Kansas has had the highest number of F5 tornadoes since 1880
- Iowa has the greatest number of F5 tornadoes per square mile
- Kentucky has the highest percentage of all tornadoes ranked as violent (F4 or F5)

Over the hills

Hills and mountains do not shelter against tornadoes – the twisters can go over them. The F4 tornado that hit the Teton Wilderness near Jackson in Wyoming, U.S., on July 21, 1987, went over mountains as high as 3,000 metres (9,843 feet), knocking down pine trees 24-30 metres (80-100 feet) tall!

Storm from the Gulf of Mexico

In late winter and early spring, tornadoes occur quite often in the states bordering the Gulf of Mexico. These tornadoes are formed when warm moist air from the Gulf of Mexico to the south and cold Arctic air just to the north collides over the Midwest and southern United States.

Chasing the Storm

Chasing storms is not a profession – it is a hobby, and an expensive one at that! People who chase storms come from all walks of life. Chasers love the challenge and adventure of trying to understand the storm, and taking photographs and videos!

▼ *Tornado chasers travel hundreds of miles from home during the tornado season*

Important equipment

A well-maintained vehicle is the most important piece of equipment because chasers often cover over 800 kilometres (497 miles) in a day. Chasers also carry cameras and camcorders, radios, scanners, miniature TVs, micro-cassette recorders, first-aid kits and road atlases. They may also have laptops, GPS tracking, anemometers and thermometers.

▼ *Storm chasers use a variety of vehicles – from sedans and vans to pickup trucks. However, sports utility vehicles (SUVs) are the favourites!*

Dangers on the road

Storm chasers must be alert to every situation and have a backup plan at hand. Strong winds can overturn a chase vehicle or blow out windows. Hail can damage vehicles and equipment, and be a traffic hazard. Flash flooding can leave chasers stranded. Besides, driving in rough weather can cause crashes.

Most 'chase-able' tornadoes

The most 'chase-able' tornadoes are those that occur during daylight and travel in open country. Also, they should not be moving too fast, and nor should they be so wrapped in clouds and rain that they are difficult to see. These types of tornadoes are most usual in Tornado Alley.

Making a contribution

Storm chasers are not professional meteorologists, but they can help the community by making reports about tornadoes to the national weather office. The photos and videos collected by chasers have often proved helpful to the science of meteorology.

INTERESTING FACT

Storm spotting is carried out by unpaid volunteers who serve their local communities. A spotter's main function is to report critical weather information to the weather office. Being a spotter is not the same thing as being a chaser, although many people choose to do both.

FACT FILE

- An estimated 1,000 storm chasers travel beyond their hometown area during any given season
- On average, chasers see a tornado once every five or ten trips
- Roger Jensen was the first person who actively hunted for tornadoes, in the upper Mid-west, U.S., in the late 1940s

The Doppler radar unit can spot a mesocyclone two to four hours before it forms into a tornado, thereby vastly aiding the science of storm forecast

Safety and Rescue

The biggest danger during a tornado is from flying debris. This accounts for a large part of the damage and many of the injuries and deaths. Although tornadoes are rare, people who live in areas where an occurrence is possible should know what to do to protect themselves.

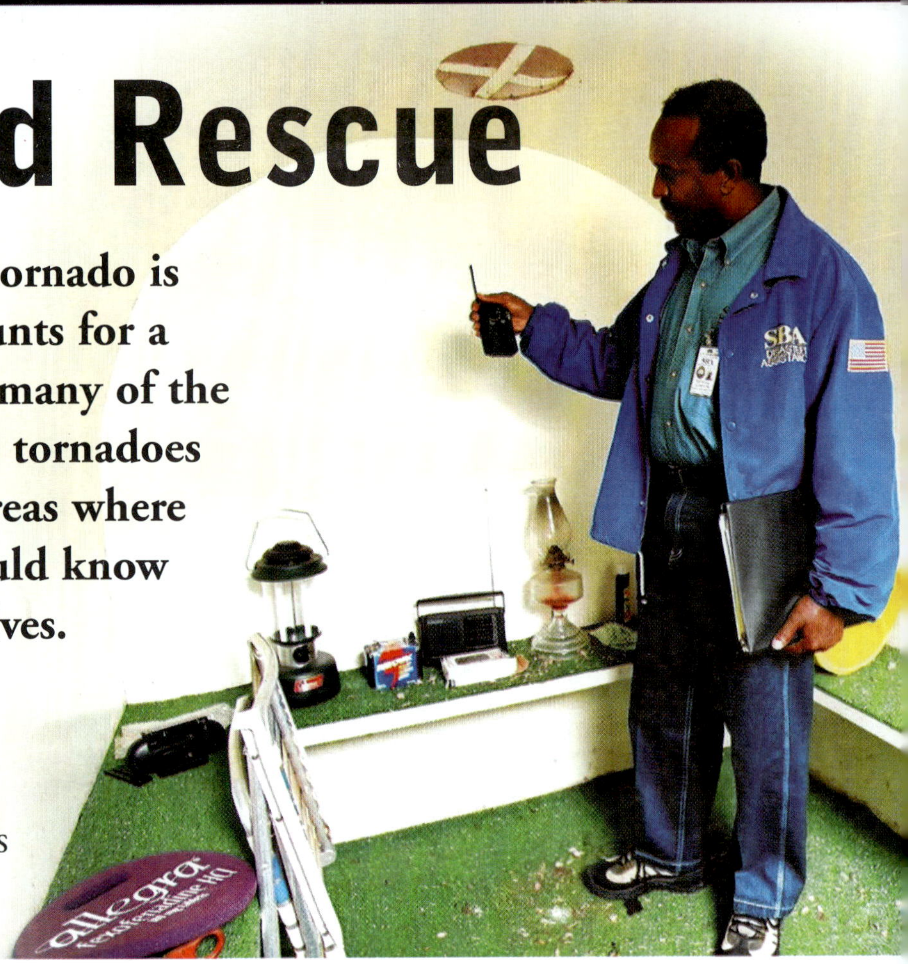

An ideal tornado shelter should include blankets, bottled water, radios and first-aid kits

Facing the storm

When conditions are right, meteorologists issue tornado watches and warnings. People also rely on weather radios, which sound an alarm even when turned off. A tornado watch sounds an alert for approaching storms. A warning means a tornado has been spotted, and people should be ready to take shelter immediately.

Storm shelter

Storm shelters are small structures made of concrete, steel, or reinforced fibreglass. They can be both above the ground or underground. Shelters must meet the set standards for construction, size and strength. They must be strong enough to protect against wind-borne debris and withstand tremendous wind pressures.

Scientists are experimenting with unique ways to control tornadoes. One of these is called cloud seeding. Here, dry ice is fed into the mesocyclone to prevent tornado formation. The idea is to force heavy rainfall and thus weaken the storm. However, the experiment is in the initial stages as yet

▲ *Search teams use dogs to assist in locating victims, saving on both time and manpower*

SAFETY AND PREPAREDNESS

- Stay calm and alert
- Seek shelter in a basement, a small closet, or a bathroom
- Stay away from windows. The broken glass can cause injuries
- Protect your body with a mattress or blankets
- Evacuate mobile homes and find shelter in a solid structure
- If you are caught on a highway, do not seek shelter under an overpass
- Do not seek shelter in a vehicle
- Do not try to outrun a tornado in your car
- Listen for reports on a portable radio
- Keep a weather radio with batteries if you live in an area with a lot of tornadoes

▲ *If you are out in the open, find a ditch or depression and lie low*

◀ *The aftermath of a tornado sees relief and rescue teams getting into intense action. The violent, spinning storm funnel can have building structures crashing down, send people and objects flying, and cause large-scale injuries and casualties*

Spinning out of Control

Today we know what tornadoes are, and that they can kill hundreds and cause immense damage. Until the mid-1900s, however, people were not aware of this destructive force. In fact, tornado forecasting and record-keeping began only in 1950. Hence, we do not have accurate information about tornadoes before that date.

▼ *The state of Missouri, U.S., has experienced some of the deadliest tornadoes in history*

The biggest outbreak

The Super Outbreak of April 3-4, 1974, was the worst tornado outbreak in U.S. history, with 148 twisters striking 13 states. The impact was felt in Canada as well. It lasted 16 hours, killing 330 people and injuring 5,484, in a damage path covering about 4,000 kilometres (2,485 miles). Seven tornadoes were rated F5 and 23 more were rated F4.

Tri-State Tornado, 1925

The Tri-State Tornado Outbreak of March 18, 1925, killed 695 people as it raced along at 96-117 km/h (60-73 mph) across the U.S. states of Missouri, Illinois and Indiana. The F5 category storm produced the most known tornado fatalities in a single city or town: at least 234 died at Murphysboro, Illinois. It remains uncertain whether it was one tornado or a 'family' of tornadoes that caused the damage.

On November 10, 2002, several tornadoes swept through the small town of Mossy Grove in Tennessee, U.S., killing eight people

Palm Sunday, April 11, 1965

The Palm Sunday Outbreak in the United States produced 51 tornadoes within a span of 12 hours. Indiana, Ohio and Michigan were the hardest hit. The tornadoes killed 256 people and caused more than $200 million in damages.

Aerial pictures of destruction in Kansas City, U.S., during the May 2003 tornado outbreak

Killer tornadoes

The United States witnessed one of its deadliest tornado outbreaks on May 4, 2003. About 84 tornadoes are said to have struck eight states, making it one of the top 10 outbreaks ever. At least 38 people were killed in Kansas, Missouri and Tennessee. The tornado onslaught continued as the twisters touched down in Oklahoma.

INTERESTING FACT

A Doppler radar mounted on a truck measured a tornado wind speed of 512 km/h (318 mph) in Moore, Oklahoma, on May 3, 1999. This was the strongest wind ever recorded near the Earth's surface. It is extremely rare to get a direct measurement of a tornado wind speed like this one, since ordinary weather instruments are blown away or broken long before winds reach these kinds of speeds. Because of this, nobody knows the highest wind speed in a tornado.

FACT FILE

- **Single month with the most tornadoes:** In the United States, the record for the most tornadoes in a month was set in May 2003 – with 516 tornadoes confirmed. This broke the old mark of 399, set in June 1992
- **Biggest known tornado:** The F4 tornado that hit the town of Hallam in Nebraska, U.S., on May 22, 2004, set a record for peak width at nearly two and half miles

The 1896 tornado that hit St. Louis, Missouri, left over 250 dead

Stormy Side Effects

Both hurricanes and tornadoes are accompanied by heavy rains, hailstorms and powerful winds. However, compared to tornadoes, hurricanes cause much more overall damage individually and over a season, and over much larger areas.

Dangers and hazards

Hurricanes can damage structures through storm surge and flooding, as well as with their strong winds. Coastal flooding is probable along low-lying areas. In comparison, tornadoes are less destructive. However, the spinning winds of powerful tornadoes can suck people and animals in, uproot trees and houses and carry off vehicles.

Heavy rains caused by hurricanes can lead to landslides, sweeping away houses and people

In the storm's wake

Storms can leave behind long-term effects that are devastating, especially in the case of hurricanes. Once the storm has passed, people in the affected area face the danger of disease epidemics. Damage to bridges, roads and railroads hinder rescue missions. Dislocated telephone lines and electricity poles result in breakdown of communication and power outages.

Storm surge

A storm surge is a rise in the ocean level caused by strong winds from a hurricane. The ocean waters sweep along the coastline near where the eye of the storm crosses the land, and can cause dangerous flooding – even in areas many miles inland.

▼ *Flash floods are the biggest threats during hurricanes. Since the water moves at a very rapid pace, rescuing victims is all the more difficult*

INTERESTING FACT

A storm surge can flood miles of coastline with devastating force. The low pressure at the centre of a hurricane causes the ocean to rise one metre (three or more feet) higher than the surrounding water. Waves, driven by wind, pile on to this bulge or dome as the system approaches land. The angle or slope of the shoreline can cause the onrushing water to rise as high as 8 metres (25 feet) above normal tide levels.

FACT FILE

- The greatest potential for loss of life during a hurricane is from the storm surge, which historically has claimed 9 out of 10 victims
- An average hurricane produces 1.5 cm/day (0.6 inch/day) of rain inside a circle of radius 665 km (360 nautical miles)
- The total energy released by a hurricane through cloud/rain formation is equivalent to 200 times the worldwide electricity-generating capacity
- The total kinetic energy (wind energy) generated by a hurricane is equivalent to about half the worldwide electricity-generating capacity

Danger at sea

Hurricanes are a threat also to sailors out at sea. Ships and boats can be tossed around, hurled against cliffs, or engulfed by waves. A small craft advisory is issued when wind speeds are between 20 and 33 knots.

Forecasting at First

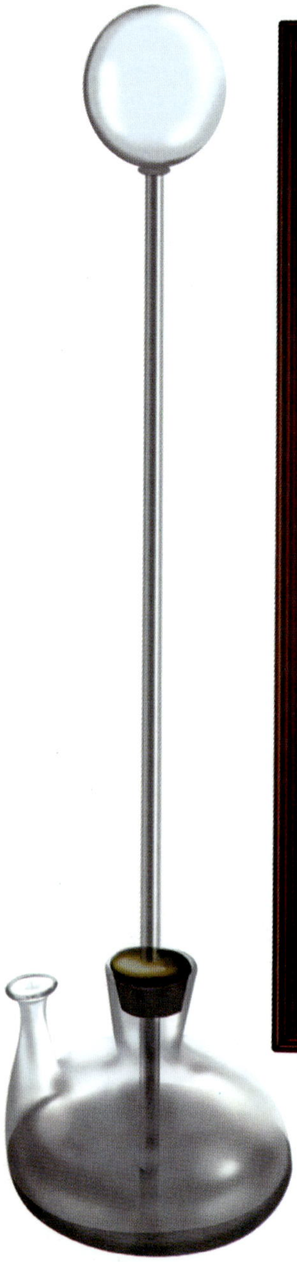

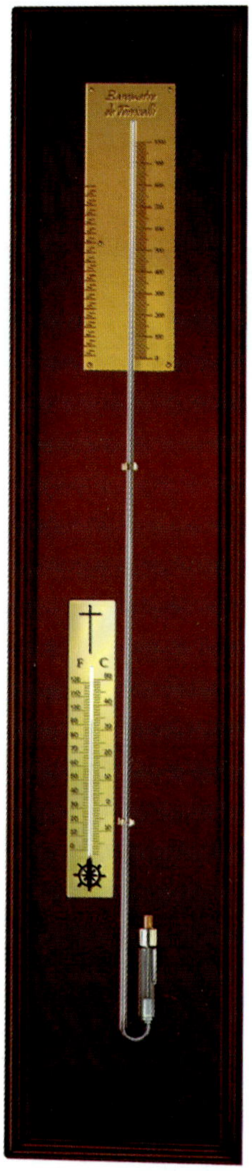

Scientists have been studying tornadoes and hurricanes for only about a hundred years. Today, with computer modelling and satellite imagery, meteorologists can track and forecast the great storms with increasing accuracy.

Early weather instruments

In ancient times, weather forecasts were made by merely observing the skies – clear skies for fair weather and black clouds for a storm! Finally, in the early 1600s, Italian scientist Galileo Galilei invented the thermoscope, an instrument that could detect temperature changes. In 1643, Galileo's pupil, Evangelista Torricelli, invented the barometer to measure the pressure of air in the atmosphere. Later, the hygrometer and the mercury thermometer helped to make weather forecast a reality.

◀ *Besides devising his mercury barometer, Torricelli also stated that changes in the atmospheric pressure led to changes in the weather*

Early forecasts

In the late 1700s, French scientist Laurent Lavoisier stated that weather could be predicted a couple of days ahead by using daily readings of atmospheric pressure, humidity, temperature, wind speed and direction. By the 20th century, equipment like the radiosonde were developed. It consists of a small box containing a thermometer, a hygrometer and a barometer. It is attached to a balloon that bursts upon reaching a certain height. The instrument collects information on temperature, pressure, humidity, and wind speed and direction.

▲ *Galileo's thermoscope showed temperature changes, though without giving exact readings*

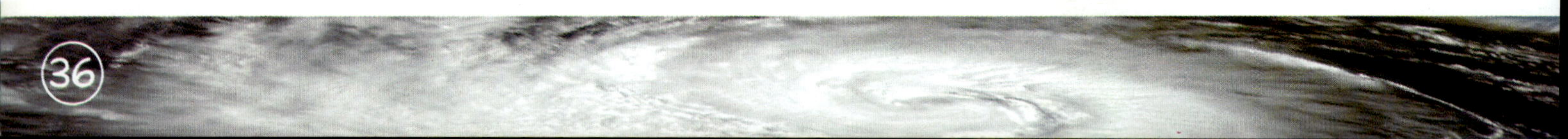

To predict a hurricane

It was in 1875 that the first successful hurricane forecast was made. Benito Vines, a Spanish priest and director of the Meteorological Observatory in Havana, Cuba, had made detailed observations about previous storms and studied the wind and cloud patterns of hurricanes. On September 11, 1875, he published his first hurricane forecast in a newspaper. His prediction helped to save several lives when the storm hit the Cuban coast two days later! Today, meteorologists use various instruments to make hurricane warnings.

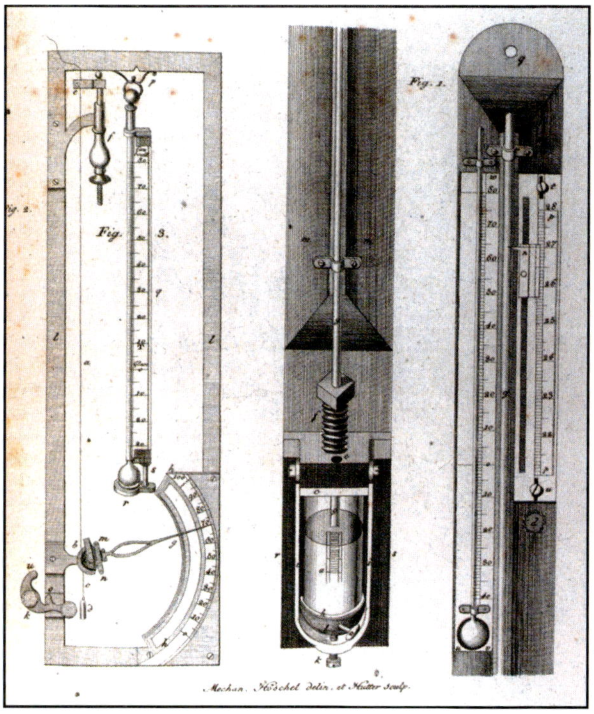

► *Traditional instruments like the thermometer and barometer are still used to predict weather conditions like hurricanes and tornadoes*

◄ *The hygrometer measures the water vapour quantity in air, thus indicating humidity levels. Air usually becomes more humid before a storm*

INTERESTING FACT

During the 1970s, scientists began mobile storm research programmes. One of these was the Totable Tornado Observatory (TOTO). It was placed in the path of a tornado to verify wind speed, direction, temperature and atmospheric pressure. However, the TOTO was often destroyed by high-speed winds, and was replaced by Doppler radars.

FACT FILE

- **1494** Christopher Columbus shelters his fleet from a tropical cyclone, and writes the first European account of a hurricane
- **1743** Ben Franklin suggests that hurricanes do not move in the same direction as the winds
- **1831** William Redfield finds that hurricane winds swirl in a counter-clockwise pattern. He begins compiling hurricane tracks
- **1875** Benito Viñes issues his first hurricane warning

Tornado forecast

It is believed that the first successful tornado forecast was made on March 25, 1948, by the U.S. Air Force Captain Robert C. Miller and Major Ernest J. Fawbush, in Oklahoma. Earlier, the Weather Bureau discouraged the use of the word 'tornado' in public forecasts. This was because they thought it might cause panic.

Forecasting and Observation

Once hurricanes and tornadoes form, scientists track their location by using various tools and instruments. But it is difficult to predict the exact path of a storm because its direction, speed and intensity can quickly change. Forecasters can only issue warnings to people in the storm's probable path.

▲ *Weather balloons, filled with helium gas, record conditions in the upper layers of the atmosphere*

Monitoring hurricanes

When hurricanes are still far out in the ocean, they are monitored mainly by satellites, and also by ships and buoys. While within 322 kilometres (200 miles) of the coast, radars provide measurements of the storms. Computer models are used to forecast storm intensity and movement.

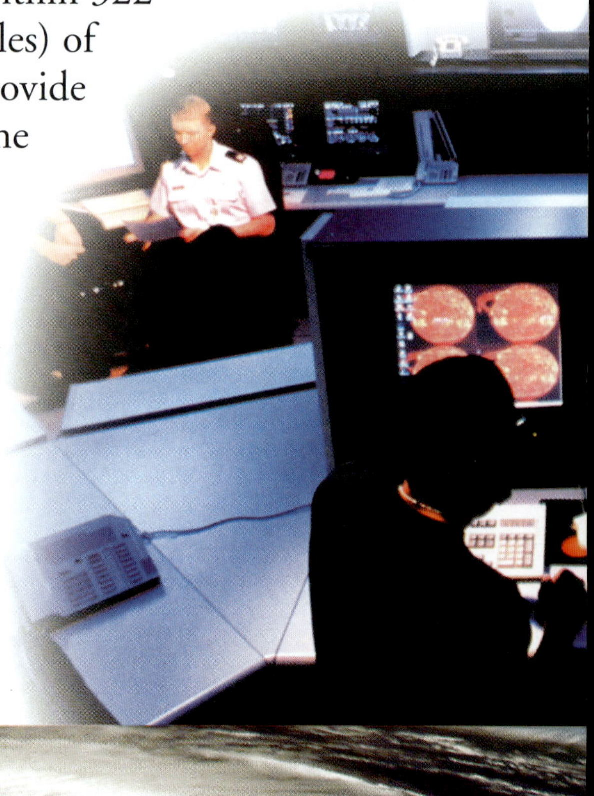

◀ *Artificial satellites are launched into space by multi-stage carrier rockets*

▲ *Geostationary weather satellites orbit over the Equator, while polar-orbiting satellites pass over the polar regions*

Eye in the sky

Radar and weather satellites are the main tools used to forecast severe weather. The Doppler weather radar can detect strong rotation within storms, and thus help forecasters make timely and specific warnings of approaching tornadoes.

When every minute counts

With advances in technology, scientists can now issue warnings before tornadoes even form. The average lead time for warnings has increased from 5-6 minutes in the early 1990s, to 10-11 minutes today.

INTERESTING FACT

The GPS dropwindsonde is a modified version of the radiosonde. It is dropped by an aircraft flying into a hurricane. The instrument uses a parachute to descend slowly through the hurricane. The dropwindsonde collects the information and radios it back to the aircraft.

FACT FILE

- Forecasters track a hurricane's movement using latitude and longitude, which can pinpoint any position on the globe
- A Doppler radar measures how fast rain or hail is moving towards or away from the radar. The farther away from the radar a storm is, the more rough the view
- In the 1980s, Doppler radars were used in warning operations as the NEXRAD (NEXt generation weather RADar) programme. NEXRAD is a computer Doppler system designed to track and analyse tornado-producing storms
- In the United States, only the National Weather Service (NWS) issues tornado forecasts nationwide

Flying into hurricanes

Aeroplanes equipped with special instruments can gather certain information that is not possible with satellites, such as surface pressure. They can find the exact centre of a storm, which may be different from what it appears to be in a satellite image. Only planes flying through the storm can tell its size, speed, direction and intensity.

Super Survivors

Imagine being caught in the middle of a severe tornado or hurricane, and living to tell the tale! Here are a few remarkable true stories of some very lucky people who survived tornadoes, lightning strikes, hurricanes and storm surges.

▲ *David Ledford of Asheville, North Carolina, U.S., and his dog, Angel, survived the wrath of Hurricane Frances in 2004*

Surviving a tornado

On December 17, 2000, an F4 tornado ripped through Tuscaloosa county in Alabama, U.S., killing 12 people and destroying over a hundred homes. But John Bibby and his wife managed to survive. About 10 years earlier, Bibby had built a makeshift underground shelter outside his house. When the warning sirens sounded on the fateful day, the couple, along with their two dogs, took refuge in the shelter.

◀ *John Bibby climbing out of his shelter*

Surviving a storm surge

Mary Ann of Mississippi survived the storm surge caused by Hurricane Camille in 1969. As the building began to collapse, Mary floated out of the window and grabbed on to anything she could find – pieces of furniture and tree branches. About 12 hours later, she was found some 6 kilometres (4 miles) from her apartment. Although severely injured, Mary recovered soon.

Surviving a lightning bolt

Gene Moore and his friends were struck by lightning while storm-chasing in Oklahoma on May 23, 1981. Luckily all of them survived. The men did not realise that they were in danger because they saw no lightning, thunder or rain, even though a tornado had touched down a mile and half way!

▲ *The tornado that struck Cordell, Oklahoma, on October 9, 2001, wreaked havoc by destroying several buildings. This local motel was one of the victims of the storm. Miraculously, though, an elderly couple survived the onslaught by standing beneath the doorframe shown in the photograph*

Surviving Hurricane Andrew

The Benitez family of Homestead, Florida, survived Hurricane Andrew in 1992 by taking shelter in a small closet. And for two days they remained standing there because it was flooded. Nor did they have anything to eat all the while, since the strong winds had blown away everything. Only three walls and the roof of their house remained by the end of the storm.

▶ *In 1999, when Hurricane Dennis struck the coasts of North Carolina, houses in Kitty Hawk remained undamaged due to their elevation*

INTERESTING FACT

Houses in hurricane areas are built in a special way to survive storms. They are raised on long stilts, looking like long-legged birds, so they are above the high water and floods that a hurricane brings. Special straps hold down the roofs during high winds. Storm shutters protect windows.

FACT FILE

- The F5 tornado that hit Xenia, Ohio, in April 1974 smashed Victor Gregory's farmhouse, but left three fragile things intact: a mirror, a case of eggs, and a box of Christmas ornaments
- A tornado picked up a baby girl from a buggy at Uren in Saskatchewan, Canada, in 1923. Hours later, she was found asleep in a shack two miles away
- In a famous incident, farmer Will Keller of Kansas was sucked into the funnel of a tornado in 1928, and survived it
- On July 1, 1955, nine-year-old SharonWeron and her horse were carried by a South Dakota tornado over a hill and across a valley, and dropped about 305 metres (1,000 feet) away

In Legend and Fiction

Greeks regarded Zeus as the god of sky and weather. He was believed to cause thunderstorms, lightning and heavy rains

The destructive power of storms like hurricanes and tornadoes inspires both fear and fascination. It's no surprise that humans throughout time have tried to control these storms. Ancient tribes were known to make offerings to the weather gods to appease them.

Weather gods around the world

People in ancient times believed that violent storms were brought on by angry weather gods. In Yoruba mythology, Oya, the female warrior, is the goddess of fire, wind and thunder. When she is angry, she creates tornadoes and hurricanes. In Egyptian legend, Set is regarded as the god of storms.

In ancient Egypt, the god Set was associated with natural calamities like hurricanes, thunderstorms, lightning, earthquakes and eclipses

Hurricanes in Mayan mythology

The Mayan people believed that when Hurakan, the god of lightning, blew his breath across the water, he brought forth dry land. Every year the Mayans threw a young woman into the sea as a sacrifice to please Hurakan. A warrior was also sacrificed to lead the girl to Hurakan's underwater kingdom.

The Bear brings winter hurricanes

In Iroquois mythology, Ga-oh is the wind giant, whose house is guarded by several animals, each representing a specific type of wind. The Bear is the north wind who brings winter hurricanes, and he can crush the world in his storms or destroy it with cold.

▲ *It is said that the approach of violent storms and winds makes horses restless, and that they start galloping at high speeds*

INTERESTING FACT

In Babylonian mythology, Marduk, the god of gods, defeated the bad-tempered goddess Tiamat with the help of a hurricane. When the other gods learned about Tiamat's plans to destroy them, they turned to Marduk for help. Armed with bows and arrows, winds and a hurricane, Marduk captured Tiamat and let the hurricane fill her jaws and stomach. Then he shot an arrow into her belly and killed her.

FACT FILE

- It was thought that a hill called Burnett's Mound protected Topeka, Kansas. However, on June 8, 1966, a violent tornado went directly over Burnett's Mound on its way into Topeka
- The first sound recording of a tornado's roar (like the sound of a freight train) was made during the 1974 Xenia tornado. Thomas Yougen turned his tape recorder on as the tornado approached the city

Tornado oddities

For a long time, people believed that tornadoes were capable of all sorts of things: sucking the water from wells, making buildings explode; or even pulling the feathers off chickens. But these 'oddities' were either lies or misunderstandings of the actual events. Another popular but misplaced belief was that tornadoes are deflected by rivers and hills.

◀ *In Aztec mythology, the serpent god Quetzalcoatl was also the god of the winds. He was also believed to have been the Sun*

▶ *Marduk became lord of all the gods after killing the dragon goddess Tiamat*

Glossary

Alert: Attentive; watchful

Broadcast: To transmit, or send out, for public use; as in a radio or television programme

Camcorder: A lightweight, hand-held television camera fitted with a video cassette recorder

Counterclockwise: In a direction opposite to the rotating hands of a clock

Critical: Serious

Curtailed: Shortened

Debris: Rubble or scattered remains of something that is broken

Density: The quality of being dense; tightly packed together

Droplet: A tiny drop

El Niño: The warming of the ocean's surface waters off the western coast of South America; occurs every 4-12 years. It causes the destruction of plankton and fish; alters storm tracks; and changes global weather patterns

Epithet: A term used to describe or characterise a person or thing

Equator: The imaginary great circle around the Earth's surface, equidistant from the poles and perpendicular to the Earth's axis of rotation. It divides the Earth into the Northern Hemisphere and the Southern Hemisphere

Evacuation: The process by which people are removed or withdrawn from a certain area

Fahrenheit: Of, or relating to, a temperature scale that registers the freezing point of water as 32°C and the boiling point as 212°C at one atmosphere of pressure

Forecast: To estimate or predict weather conditions in advance, using methods of scientific analysis

Geophysicist: A scientist who studies the physics of the Earth and its environment, including the physics behind fields like meteorology and seismology

Gravity: The force of attraction that pulls bodies toward the centre of a celestial body, such as the Earth

Hailstone: Small pellet of ice that falls during a hailstorm

Hemisphere: Either the northern or southern half of the Earth as divided by the Equator; or the eastern or western half as divided by a meridian

Hinder: To obstruct

Humidity: Dampness; amount of water vapour in the atmosphere

Imminent: About to happen

Inland: Located in the interior part of a country or a region

Intensity: Amount of power or force

Kinetic energy: Energy possessed by a body in motion

La Niña: The cooling of the ocean surface off the western coast of South America, affecting weather patterns; opposite of El Nino.

Low-lying area: Regions that lie very close to sea level, or of very little elevation above the ground

Microsecond: One millionth of a second; one thousandth of a millisecond

Molecule: The smallest particle of a substance that retains the chemical and physical properties of the substance, and is composed of two or more atoms; a group of like or different atoms held together by chemical forces

Precipitation: Any form of water – like rain, hail or snow – that falls on the Earth's surface

Radar: The equipment used to locate distant objects by reflecting high-frequency radio waves off the surface of the object

Recycle: To put or pass through a cycle again, as for further treatment

Richter scale: A scale used to measure the intensity of an earthquake

Stilt: Long pole or pillar used to support a house or a building

Surge: A heavy billowing or swelling motion like that of great waves

Tilt: To cause to slope by raising one end; incline

Uproot: To pull up from the ground (such as a plant and its roots); to displace

Volunteer: A person who offers to perform a service, especially for the needy, of his or her own free will

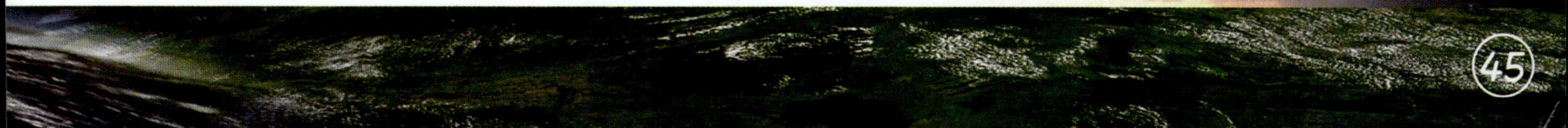